CATS ARE SMARTER THAN MEN, TOO!

CATS ARE SMARTER THAN MEN, TOO!

By Beverly Guhl

Hodder & Stoughton

First published in Great Britain in 1995
by Hodder & Stoughton
A division of Hodder Headline PLC

10 9 8 7 6 5 4 3 2 1

A CIP catalogue record for this title is available from the British Library

ISBN 0-340-64943-7

Printed and bound in Great Britain by
Mackays of Chatham PLC, Chatham, Kent

Hodder and Stoughton Ltd
A division of Hodder Headline PLC
338 Euston Road
London NW1 3BH

To Gary Brim with love and laughter . . .
Bev, Nunu and Hobie

Beverly Guhl has designed and marketed everything from greeting cards and stationery to decorative magnets, record albums, and mugs. She is the author of *Cats are Better than Men*. The mother of two college-age children, she lives in Texas with her husband, who is almost as smart as her two cats. Although a staunch supporter of human rights and gender equality, she says she would probably vote for a cat if one ran for office.

CATS ARE SMARTER THAN MEN, TOO!

They never ask if you've
gained weight.

You never have to ask
them to take a bath.

They'd never say,
"You call this dinner?"

🐾

They know better than
to argue with you.

They never ask you to wear
spike heels and a tight
sheath dress.

Their love isn't dependent
on how clean the house is.

They'd never ask you to wear a padded bra.

🐾

They understand the difference between laziness and a beauty nap.

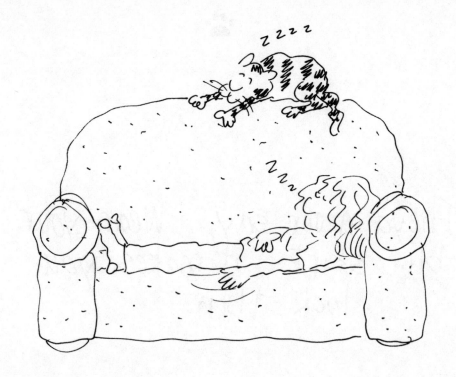

They'd never say, "Wear your
blue skirt — it makes you
look thin."

They don't drool over other
women.

They'd never ask, "How much did that cost me?"

They'd never say, "You did WHAT to the car?"

You can trust them with
your best friend.

They'd never say, "Move, honey, you're blocking the T.V.!"

They think you're very intelligent.

They'd never ask, "So, what
have you been doing all day?"

They never insist on watching
T.V. while eating dinner.

They appreciate and understand the importance of affection.

They aren't aggravated by
instruction manuals.

They'd never ask, "Are you sure you want to eat that?"

They don't sleep through things
that go bump in the night.

They don't make you feel
bad when you don't exercise.

They never accidentally call you
by an old girlfriend's name.

They would never wear white socks with a business suit.

They know the importance of punctuality.

They would never use your toothbrush.

They don't put empty containers back in the refrigerator.

They don't run up huge
debts on charge cards.

They love being helpful.

They stop using the bathroom
when it's dirty.

They'd never give you an
appliance for your birthday.

They're not dependent on
you for all their meals.

They agree with everything
you say.

They'd never say, "Why can't you look like _that_?"

They always appreciate your
efforts in the kitchen.

They never question how much
money you spend on phone calls.

They don't have "platonic"
female friends who look
like movie stars.

They don't try to
psychoanalyze you.

They never tell you what to do,
when to do it, or how to do it.

They're always sincere.

They don't try to fix
things themselves.

They never make you cry.

They don't ask you to
wear erotic lingerie.

They love it when your
thighs get fat.

They aren't interested in
you only for your body.

They still love you even
when you're moody.

They don't make fun of your taste in music, television shows, books, or anything else.

They think using a map on
a road trip is a good idea.

They're not too proud to ask you for help when they need it.

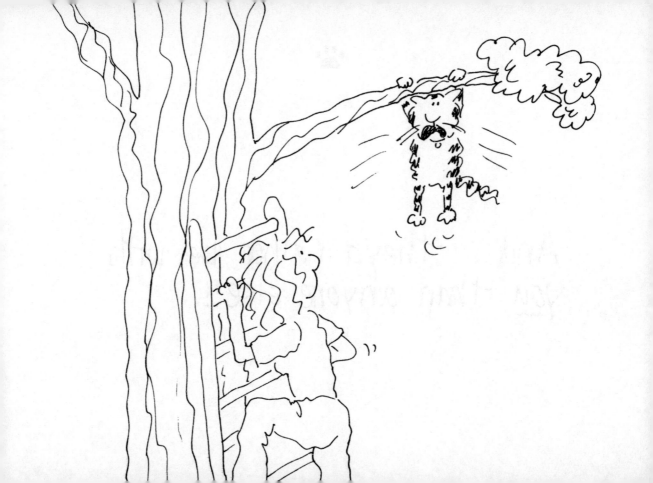

And... they'd rather be with
you than anyone else!!